Still L.

A Play in Five Scenes

from

Tonight at 8:30

by Noël Coward

A SAMUEL FRENCH ACTING EDITION

SAMUEL FRENCH

FOUNDED 1830

New York Hollywood London Toronto

SAMUELFRENCH.COM

ISBN   978-0-573-62490-2   Printed   in   U.S.A.   #1002

IMPORTANT BILLING AND CREDIT REQUIREMENTS

STILL LIFE

Produced at the Phœnix Theatre, Charing Cross Road, London, W.C.2, in January, 1936, with the following cast of Characters :

LAURA JESSON	.	.	.	.	.	*Gertrude Lawrence.*
MYRTLE BAGOT	.	.	.	.	.	*Joyce Carey.*
BERYL WATERS	.	.	.	.	.	*Moya Nugent.*
STANLEY	.	.	.	.	.	*Kenneth Carten.*
ALBERT GODBY	.	.	.	.	.	*Alan Webb.*
ALEC HARVEY	.	.	.	.	.	*Noel Coward.*
YOUNG MAN	.	.	.	.	.	*Charles Peters.*
BILL	.	.	.	.	.	*Edward Underdown.*
JOHNNIE	.	.	.	.	.	*Anthony Pelissier.*
MILDRED	.	.	.	.	.	*Betty Hare.*
DOLLY MESSITER	.	.	.	.	.	*Everley Gregg.*

The action of the Play takes place in the refreshment-room of Milford Junction Station.

TIME.—The present.

STILL LIFE

Produced by John C. Wilson at the National Theatre in New York City on November 30, 1936, as one of a series of nine one-act plays by Noel Coward, under the title of "TO-NIGHT AT EIGHT-THIRTY." The play was directed by the author and the cast was as follows:

LAURA JESSON	*Gertrude Lawrence.*
MYRTLE BAGOT	*Joyce Carey.*
BERYL WATERS	*Moya Nugent.*
STANLEY	*Kenneth Carten.*
ALBERT GODBY	*Alan Webb.*
ALEC HARVEY	*Noel Coward.*
YOUNG MAN	*Charles Peters.*
BILL	*Edward Underdown.*
JOHNNIE	*Anthony Pelissier.*
MILDRED	*Betty Hare.*
DOLLY MESSITER	*Joan Swinstead.*

The action of the play takes place in the refreshment room of Milford Junction Station.

TIME.—The Present.

STILL LIFE

SCENE I

The SCENE *is the refreshment-room of Milford Junction Station.*

On the right of the stage is a curved counter piled with glass cases containing sandwiches, rock-cakes, etc. There are rows of teacups and glasses symmetrically arranged, an expression of the fanciful side of MYRTLE'S *imagination. Schweppes' bottles of soda and Tonic water have been placed in circles and squares. Even the rock-cakes mount each other on the glass stands in a disciplined pattern. There is a metal machine which gushes hot tea, a sort of cylindrical samovar.*

For drinking hours there are the usual appurtenances for the drawing of draught beer, and the wall behind the counter, except for a door up stage, is lined with looking-glass shelves supporting bottles, packets of chocolate, packets of cigarettes, etc.

There are two windows in the left wall. Between them is a door leading on to the platform. There is a table against the back wall, a stove in the corner, and two more tables against the left-hand wall. There are several advertisements and calendars in frames, and on each table is a vase containing very bright artificial flowers.

MYRTLE BAGOT *herself is a buxom and imposing widow. Her hair is piled high, and her expression reasonably jaunty, except on those occasions when her strong sense of refinement gets the better of her.* BERYL WATERS, *her assistant, is pretty but dimmed, not only by* MYRTLE'S *personal effulgence, but by her firm authority.*

When the CURTAIN *rises it is about* 5.25 *p.m. on an evening in April. The evening sunlight streams through the left-hand windows, illuminating gaily the paraphernalia on the counter.*

A YOUNG MAN *in a mackintosh is finishing his tea at the upstage* C. *table and reading an evening paper.* LAURA JESSON *is sitting at the downstage tab'e, having tea. She is an attractive woman in the thirties. Her clothes are not particularly smart, but obviously chosen with taste. She looks exactly what she is—a pleasant, ordinary married woman, rather pale, for she is not very strong, and with the definite charm of personality which comes from natural kindliness, humour and reasonable conscience. She is reading a Boots library book at which she occasionally smiles. On the chair beside her there are several parcels, as she has been shopping.*

STANLEY *enters from the platform. He wears a seedy green uniform and carries a tray strapped to his shoulders. He goes to the counter. He addresses* MYRTLE *with becoming respect;* BERYL, *however, he winks at lewdly whenever the opportunity occurs.*

STANLEY. I'm out of " Maries ", Mrs. Bagot, and I could do with some more Nestlé's plain.

MYRTLE (*scrutinizing the tray*). Let me see.

STANLEY. An old girl on the four-ten asked if I'd got an ice-cream wafer. I didn't 'arf laugh.

MYRTLE. I don't see that there was anything to laugh at—a very natural request on a faine day.

STANLEY. What did she think I was—a " Stop me and buy one " !

(BERYL *sniggers.*)

MYRTLE. Be quiet, Beryl—and as for you, Stanley, don't you be saucy. You were saucy when you started to work here, and you've been getting saucier and saucier ever since. Here you are—— (*She gives him some packets of biscuits and Nestlé's chocolate.*) Go on, now.

STANLEY (*cheerfully*). All right ! All right !

(*He winks at* BERYL *and goes out.*)

MYRTLE. And see here, Beryl Waters, I'll trouble you to remember you're on duty——

BERYL. I didn't do anything.

MYRTLE. Exactly—you just stand there giggling like a fool. Did you make out that list ?

BERYL. Yes, Mrs. Bagot.

MYRTLE. Where is it ?

BERYL. I put it on your desk.

MYRTLE. Where's your cloth ?

BERYL. Here, Mrs. Bagot.

MYRTLE. Well, go and clean off Number Three. I can see the crumbs on it from here.

BERYL. It's them rock-cakes.

MYRTLE. Never you mind about the rock-cakes ; just you do as you're told and don't argue.

(BERYL *goes to clean the table up* L. ALBERT GODBY *enters. He is a ticket inspector, somewhere between thirty and forty. His accent is North Country.*)

ALBERT. Hullo ! Hullo ! Hullo !

MYRTLE. Quite a stranger, aren't you ?

ALBERT. I couldn't get in yesterday.

MYRTLE (*bridling*). I wondered what had happened to you.

ALBERT. I 'ad a bit of a dust-up.

MYRTLE (*preparing his tea*). What about ?

ALBERT. Saw a chap getting out of a first-class compartment, and when he come to give up 'is ticket it was third class, and I told 'im he'd 'ave to pay excess, and then he turned a bit nasty and I 'ad to send for Mr. Saunders.

MYRTLE. Fat lot of good he'd be.

ALBERT. He ticked him off proper.

MYRTLE. Seein's believing——

ALBERT. He's not a bad lot, Mr. Saunders ; after all, you can't expect much spirit from a man who's only got one lung and a wife with diabetes.

MYRTLE. I thought something must be wrong when you didn't come.

ALBERT. I'd have popped in to explain, but I

had a date and 'ad to run for it the moment I went off.

MYRTLE (*frigidly*). Oh, indeed !

ALBERT. A chap I know's getting married.

MYRTLE. Very interesting, I'm sure.

ALBERT. What's up with you, anyway ?

MYRTLE. I'm sure I don't know to what you're referring.

ALBERT. You're a bit unfriendly all of a sudden.

MYRTLE (*ignoring him*). Beryl, hurry up—put some coal in the stove while you're at it.

BERYL. Yes, Mrs. Bagot.

MYRTLE. I'm afraid I really can't stand here wasting my time in idle gossip, Mr. Godby.

ALBERT. Aren't you going to offer me another cup ?

MYRTLE. You can 'ave another cup and welcome when you've finished that one. Beryl'll give it to you —I've got my accounts to do.

ALBERT. I'd rather you gave it to me.

MYRTLE. Time and taide wait for no man, Mr. Godby.

ALBERT. I don't know what you're huffy about, but whatever it is I'm very sorry.

MYRTLE. You misunderstand me—I'm not——

(ALEC HARVEY *enters. He is about thirty-five. He wears a moustache, a mackintosh and a squash hat, and he carries a small bag. His manner is decisive and un-flurried.*)

ALEC. A cup of tea, please.

MYRTLE. Certainly. (*She pours it out in silence.*) Cake or pastry ?

ALEC. No, thank you.

MYRTLE. Threepence.

ALEC (*paying*). Thank you.

(*He takes his cup of tea and goes over to the table up* L. *He takes off his hat and sits down.* LAURA *glances at the clock, collects her parcels in a leisurely manner and goes out on to the platform.* BERYL *returns to her place behind the counter.*)

BERYL. Minnie hasn't touched her milk.

MYRTLE. Did you put it down for her ?

BERYL. Yes, but she never came in for it.

MYRTLE. Go out the back and see if she's in the yard.

(BERYL *goes.*)

ALBERT (*conversationally*). Fond of animals ?

MYRTLE. In their place.

ALBERT. My landlady's got a positive mania for animals—she's got two cats, one Manx and one ordinary ; three rabbits in a hutch in the kitchen, they belong to her little boy by rights ; and one of them foolish-looking dogs with hair over his eyes.

MYRTLE. I don't know to what breed you refer.

ALBERT. I don't think it knows itself——

(*There is a rumbling noise in the distance, and the sound of a bell.*)

MYRTLE. There's the boat train.

(*There is a terrific clatter as the express roars through the station.*)

ALBERT. What about my other cup ?—I shall have to be moving—the five forty-three will be in in a minute.

MYRTLE. Who's on the gate ? (*She pours him out another cup.*)

ALBERT. Young William.

MYRTLE. You're neglecting your duty, you know—that's what you're doing.

ALBERT. A bit of relaxation never did anyone any harm——

(LAURA *enters hurriedly, holding a handkerchief to her eye.*)

LAURA. Please could you give me a glass of water ? I've got something in my eye and I want to bathe it.

MYRTLE. Would you like me to have a look ?

LAURA. Please don't trouble. I think the water will do it.

MYRTLE (*handing her a glass of water*). Here.

(MYRTLE *and* ALBERT *watch her in silence as she bathes her eye.*)

ALBERT. Bit of coal-dust, I expect.

MYRTLE. A man I knew lost the sight of one eye through getting a bit of grit in it.

ALBERT. Nasty thing—very nasty.

MYRTLE (*as* LAURA *lifts her head*). Better ?

LAURA (*obviously in pain*). I'm afraid not—Oh !

(ALEC *rises from his table and comes over.*)

ALEC. Can I help you ?

LAURA. Oh, no, please—it's only something in my eye.

MYRTLE. Try pulling down your eyelid as far as it'll go.

ALBERT. And then blowing your nose.

ALEC. Please let me look. I happen to be a doctor.

LAURA. It's very kind of you.

ALEC. Turn round to the light, please—now—look up—now look down—I can see it. Keep still—— (*He twists up the corner of his handkerchief and rapidly operates with it.*) There——

LAURA (*blinking*). Oh, dear—what a relief—it was agonizing.

ALEC. It looks like a bit of grit.

LAURA. It was when the express went through. Thank you very much indeed——

ALEC. Not at all.

(*There is the sound of a bell on the platform.*)

ALBERT (*gulping down his tea*). There we go—I must run.

LAURA. How lucky for me that you happened to be here.

ALEC. Anybody could have done it.

LAURA. Never mind, you did, and I'm most grateful. There's my train.—Good-bye.

(*She puts out her hand and* ALEC *shakes it politely. She goes out, followed at a run by* ALBERT GODBY. ALEC *looks after her for a moment and then goes back to his table. There is the noise of the train rumbling into the station as the lights fade.*)

SCENE II

The SCENE *is the same and the time is about the same.
Nearly three months have passed since the preceding
scene, and it is now July.*

MYRTLE *is resplendent in a light overall ;* BERYL'S *appearance is unaltered. The tables are all unoccupied.*

MYRTLE (*slightly relaxed in manner*).   It's all very fane,
I said, expecting me to do this, that and the other, but
what do *I* get out of it ?   You can't expect me to be a
cook-housekeeper and char rolled into one during the
day, and a loving wife in the evening, just because you
feel like it.—Oh, dear, no.   There are just as good fish in
the sea, I said, as ever came out of it, and I packed my
boxes then and there and left him.

BERYL.   Didn't you ever go back ?

MYRTLE.   Never.   I went to my sister's place at
Folkestone for a bit, and then I went in with a friend of
mine and we opened a tea-shop in Hythe.

BERYL.   And what happened to him ?

MYRTLE.   Dead as a doornail inside three years.

BERYL.   Well, I never !

MYRTLE.   So you see, every single thing she told me
came true—first, them clubs coming together, an unexpected journey ; then the Queen of Diamonds and the ten
—that was my friend and the tea-shop business ; then
the Ace of Spades three times running——

(STANLEY *enters.*)

STANLEY.   Two rock and an apple.

MYRTLE.   What for ?

STANLEY.   Party on the up platform.

MYRTLE.   Why can't they come in here for them ?

STANLEY.   Ask me another.   (*He winks at* BERYL.)

MYRTLE.   Got something in your eye ?

STANLEY.   Nothing beyond a bit of a twinkle every
now and again.

BERYL (*giggling*).   Oh, you are awful !

MYRTLE.   You learn to behave yourself, my lad.

Here are your rock-cakes. Beryl, stop sniggering and give me an apple off the stand.

(BERYL *complies.*)

Not off the front, silly; haven't you got any sense ?— Here—— (*She takes one from the back of the stand so as to leave the symmetry undisturbed.*)

STANLEY. This one's got a hole in it.

MYRTLE. Tell 'em to come and choose for themselves if they're particular—go on, now.

STANLEY. All right—give us a chance.

MYRTLE. What people want to eat on the platform for I really don't know. Tell Mr. Godby not to forget his tea.

STANLEY. Righto !

(*He goes out as* ALEC *and* LAURA *come in.* LAURA *is wearing a summer dress,* ALEC *a grey flannel suit.*)

ALEC. Tea or lemonade ?

LAURA. Tea, I think—it's more refreshing, really. (*She sits at the table down* L.)

(ALEC *goes to the counter.*)

ALEC. Two teas, please.

MYRTLE. Cakes or pastry ?

ALEC (*to* LAURA). Cakes or pastry ?

LAURA. No, thank you.

ALEC. Are those Bath buns fresh ?

MYRTLE. Certainly they are—made this morning.

ALEC. Two, please.

(MYRTLE *puts two Bath buns on a plate. Meanwhile* BERYL *has drawn two cups of tea.*)

MYRTLE. That'll be eightpence.

ALEC. All right. (*He pays her.*)

MYRTLE. Take the tea to the table, Beryl.

ALEC. I'll carry the buns.

(BERYL *brings the tea to the table.* ALEC *follows with the buns.*)

You must eat one of these—fresh this morning.

LAURA. Very fattening.

ALEC. I don't hold with such foolishness.

(BERYL *returns to the counter*.)

MYRTLE. I'm going over my accounts. Let me know when Albert comes in.

BERYL. Yes, Mrs. Bagot.

(MYRTLE *goes off* R. BERYL *settles down behind the counter with "Peg's Paper.")*

LAURA. They do look good, I must say.

ALEC. One of my earliest passions—I've never outgrown it.

LAURA. Do you like milk in your tea ?

ALEC. Yes, don't you ?

LAURA. Yes—fortunately.

ALEC. Station refreshments are generally a wee bit arbitrary, you know.

LAURA. I wasn't grumbling.

ALEC (*smiling*). Do you ever grumble—are you ever sullen and cross and bad-tempered ?

LAURA. Of course I am—at least, not sullen exactly —but I sometimes get into rages.

ALEC. I can't visualize you in a rage.

LAURA. I really don't see why you should.

ALEC. Oh, I don't know—there are signs, you know —one can usually tell——

LAURA. Long upper lips and jaw-lines and eyes close together ?

ALEC. You haven't any of those things.

LAURA. Do you feel guilty at all ? I do.

ALEC (*smiling*). Guilty ?

LAURA. You ought to more than me, really—you neglected your work this afternoon.

ALEC. I worked this morning—a little relaxation never did anyone any harm. Why should either of us feel guilty ?

LAURA. I don't know—a sort of instinct—as though we were letting something happen that oughtn't to happen.

ALEC. How awfully nice you are!

LAURA. When I was a child in Cornwall—we lived in Cornwall, you know—May, that's my sister, and I used to climb out of our bedroom window on summer nights and go down to the cove and bathe. It was dreadfully cold, but we felt very adventurous. I'd never have dared do it by myself, but sharing the danger made it all right—that's how I feel now, really.

ALEC. Eat up your bun—it's awfully bad for you.

LAURA. You're laughing at me!

ALEC. Yes, a little, but I'm laughing at myself too.

LAURA. Why?

ALEC. For feeling a small pang when you said about being guilty.

LAURA. There you are, you see!

ALEC. We haven't done anything wrong.

LAURA. Of course we haven't.

ALEC. An accidental meeting—then another accidental meeting—then a little lunch—then the movies—what could be more ordinary? More natural?

LAURA. We're adults, after all.

ALEC. I never see myself as an adult, do you?

LAURA (*firmly*). Yes, I do. I'm a respectable married woman with a husband and a home and three children.

ALEC. But there must be a part of you, deep down inside, that doesn't feel like that at all—some little spirit that still wants to climb out of the window—that still longs to splash about a bit in the dangerous sea.

LAURA. Perhaps we none of us ever grow up entirely.

ALEC. How awfully nice you are!

LAURA. You said that before.

ALEC. I thought perhaps you hadn't heard.

LAURA. I heard all right.

ALEC (*gently*). I'm respectable too, you know. I have a home and a wife and children and responsibilities —I also have a lot of work to do and a lot of ideals all mixed up with it.

LAURA. What's she like?

ALEC. Madeleine?

LAURA. Yes.

ALEC. Small, dark, rather delicate——

LAURA. How funny! I should have thought she'd be fair.

ALEC. And your husband? What's he like?

LAURA. Medium height, brown hair, kindly, unemotional and not delicate at all.

ALEC. You said that proudly.

LAURA. Did I? (*She looks down.*)

ALEC. What's the matter?

LAURA. The matter? What could be the matter?

ALEC. You suddenly went away.

LAURA (*brightly*). I thought perhaps we were being rather silly.

ALEC. Why?

LAURA. Oh, I don't know—we are such complete strangers, really.

ALEC. It's one thing to close a window, but quite another to slam it down on my fingers.

LAURA. I'm sorry.

ALEC. Please come back again.

LAURA. Is tea bad for one? Worse than coffee, I mean?

ALEC. If this is a professional interview, my fee is a guinea.

LAURA (*laughing*). It's nearly time for your train.

ALEC. I hate to think of it, chugging along, interrupting our tea-party.

LAURA. I really am sorry now.

ALEC. What for?

LAURA. For being disagreeable.

ALEC. I don't think you could be disagreeable.

LAURA. You said something just now about your work and ideals being mixed up with it—what ideals?

ALEC. That's a long story.

LAURA. I suppose all doctors ought to have ideals, really—otherwise I should think the work would be unbearable.

ALEC. Surely you're not encouraging me to talk shop?

LAURA. Do you come here every Thursday?

**

ALEC. Yes. I come in from Churley, and spend a day in the hospital. Stephen Lynn graduated with me —he's the chief physician here. I take over from him once a week; it gives him a chance to go up to London and me a chance to observe and study the hospital patients.

LAURA. Is that a great advantage?

ALEC. Of course. You see, I have a special pigeon.

LAURA. What is it?

ALEC. Preventive medicine.

LAURA. Oh, I see.

ALEC (*laughing*). I'm afraid you don't.

LAURA. I was trying to be intelligent.

ALEC. Most good doctors, especially when they're young, have private dreams—that's the best part of them; sometimes, though, those get over-professionalized and strangulated and—am I boring you?

LAURA. No—I don't quite understand—but you're not boring me.

ALEC. What I mean is this—all good doctors must be primarily enthusiasts. They must have, like writers and painters and priests, a sense of vocation—a deep-rooted, unsentimental desire to do good.

LAURA. Yes—I see that.

ALEC. Well, obviously one way of preventing disease is worth fifty ways of curing it—that's where my ideal comes in—preventive medicine isn't anything to do with medicine at all, really—it's concerned with conditions, living conditions and common sense and hygiene. For instance, my speciality is pneumoconiosis.

LAURA. Oh, dear!

ALEC. Don't be alarmed, it's simpler than it sounds —it's nothing but a slow process of fibrosis of the lung due to the inhalation of particles of dust. In the hospital here there are splendid opportunities for observing cures and making notes, because of the coal-mines.

LAURA. You suddenly look much younger.

ALEC (*brought up short*). Do I?

LAURA. Almost like a little boy.

ALEC. What made you say that?

LAURA (*staring at him*). I don't know—yes, I do.

ALEC (*gently*). Tell me.

LAURA (*with panic in her voice*). Oh, no—I couldn't, really. You were saying about the coal-mines——

ALEC (*looking into her eyes*). Yes—the inhalation of coal-dust—that's one specific form of the diseases—it's called anthracosis.

LAURA (*hypnotized*). What are the others ?

ALEC. Chalicosis—that comes from metal dust—steel-works, you know——

LAURA. Yes, of course. Steel-works.

ALEC. And silicosis—stone dust—that's gold-mines.

LAURA (*almost in a whisper*). I see.

(*There is the sound of a bell.*)

There's your train.

ALEC (*looking down*). Yes.

LAURA. You mustn't miss it.

ALEC. No.

LAURA (*again the panic in her voice*). What's the matter ?

ALEC (*with an effort*). Nothing—nothing at all.

LAURA (*socially*). It's been so very nice—I've enjoyed my afternoon enormously.

ALEC. I'm so glad—so have I. I apologize for boring you with those long medical words——

LAURA. I feel dull and stupid, not to be able to understand more.

ALEC. Shall I see you again ?

(*There is the sound of a train approaching.*)

LAURA. It's the other platform, isn't it ? You'll have to run. Don't worry about me—mine's due in a few minutes.

ALEC. Shall I see you again ?

LAURA. Of course—perhaps you could come over to Ketchworth one Sunday. It's rather far, I know, but we should be delighted to see you.

ALEC (*intensely*). Please—please——

(The train is heard drawing to a standstill.)

LAURA.   What is it ?
ALEC.   Next Thursday—the same time——
LAURA.   No—I can't possibly—I——
ALEC.   Please—I ask you most humbly——
LAURA.   You'll miss your train !
ALEC.   All right.   (*He gets up.*)
LAURA.   Run——
ALEC (*taking her hand*).   Good-bye.
LAURA (*breathlessly*).   I'll be there.
ALEC.   Thank you, my dear.

(He goes out at a run, colliding with ALBERT GODBY, *who
is on his way in.)*

ALBERT.   'Ere—'ere—take it easy now—take it easy
——   (*He goes over to the counter.*)

*(*LAURA *sits quite still, staring in front of her as the lights
fade.)*

SCENE III

*It is now October.   Three months have passed since the
preceding scene.*

The refreshment-room is empty except for MYRTLE, *who
is bending down putting coal into the stove.*

ALBERT GODBY *enters.   Upon perceiving her slightly
vulnerable position, he slaps her lightly on the behind—
she springs to her feet.*

MYRTLE.   Albert Godby, how dare you !
ALBERT.   I couldn't resist it.
MYRTLE.   I'll trouble you to keep your hands to
yourself.
ALBERT.   You're blushing—you look wonderful when
you're angry, like an avenging angel.

MYRTLE. I'll give you avenging angel—coming in here taking liberties——

ALBERT. I didn't think after what you said last Monday you'd object to a friendly little slap.

MYRTLE. Never you mind about last Monday—I'm on duty now. A nice thing if Mr. Saunders had happened to be looking through the window.

ALBERT. If Mr. Saunders is in the 'abit of looking through windows, it's time he saw something worth looking at.

MYRTLE. You ought to be ashamed of yourself!

ALBERT. It's just high spirits—don't be mad at me.

MYRTLE. High spirits indeed!

ALBERT (*singing*). "I'm twenty-one to-day—I'm twenty-one to-day.
I've got the key of the parlour door—
I've never been twenty-one before——"

MYRTLE (*retiring behind the counter*). Don't make such a noise—they'll hear you on the platform.

ALBERT (*singing*). "Picture you upon my knee, and tea for two and two for tea."

MYRTLE. Now look here, Albert Godby—once and for all, will you behave yourself!

ALBERT (*singing*). "Sometimes I'm 'appy—sometimes I'm blue-oo——" (*He breaks off.*) This is one of my 'appy moments——

MYRTLE. Here, take your tea and be quiet.

ALBERT. It's all your fault, anyway.

MYRTLE. I don't know to what you're referring, I'm sure.

ALBERT. I was thinking of to-night——

MYRTLE. If you don't learn to behave yourself there won't be a to-night—or any other night, either——

ALBERT (*singing*). "I'm in love again and the spring is coming.
I'm in love again, hear my heart-strings humming——"

MYRTLE. Will you hold your noise?

ALBERT. Give us a kiss.

MYRTLE. I'll do no such thing.

ALBERT. Just a quick one—across the counter. (*He grabs her arm across the counter.*)

MYRTLE. Albert, stop it !

ALBERT. Come on—there's a love.

MYRTLE. Let go of me this minute.

ALBERT. Come on, just one.

(*They scuffle for a moment, upsetting a neat pile of cakes on to the floor.*)

MYRTLE. Now look at me Banburys—all over the floor.

(ALBERT *bends down to pick them up.* STANLEY *enters.*)

STANLEY. Just in time—or born in the vestry.

MYRTLE. You shut your mouth and help Mr. Godby pick up them cakes.

STANLEY. Anything to oblige. (*He helps* ALBERT.)

(ALEC *and* LAURA *come in.* LAURA *goes to their usual table.* ALEC *goes to the counter.*)

ALEC. Good afternoon.

MYRTLE (*grandly*). Good afternoon.

ALEC. Two teas, please.

MYRTLE. Cake or pastry ?

ALEC. No, thank you—just the tea.

ALBERT (*conversationally*). Nice weather.

ALEC. Very nice.

ALBERT. Bit of a nip in the air, though.

(MYRTLE, *having given* ALEC *two cups of tea, and taken the money for it, turns to* STANLEY.)

MYRTLE. What are you standing there gaping at ?

STANLEY. Where's Beryl ?

MYRTLE. Never you mind about Beryl ; you ought to be on Number Four, and well you know it.

ALBERT (*reflectively*). Love's young dream !

(ALEC, *meanwhile, has carried the two cups of tea over to the table and sat down.*)

STANLEY. There's been a run on the Cadbury's nut milk this afternoon! I shall need some more.

MYRTLE (*looking at his tray*). How many have you got left?

STANLEY. Only three.

MYRTLE. Take six more then, and don't forget to mark 'em down.

STANLEY. Righto.

(STANLEY *goes behind the counter and collects six packets of chocolate, then he goes out whistling.*)

ALEC. I didn't mean to be unkind.

LAURA. It doesn't matter.

(*A* YOUNG MAN *comes in and goes to the counter.*)

YOUNG MAN. Cup of coffee, please, and a beef sandwich.

MYRTLE. We're out of beef—will ham do?

YOUNG MAN. Yes—ham'll do.

(ALBERT *winks at* MYRTLE *over his tea-cup.* MYRTLE *draws a cup of coffee for the* YOUNG MAN *and takes a sandwich out of one of the glass stands.*)

ALEC. We can't part like this.

LAURA. I think it would be better if we did.

ALEC. You don't really mean that?

LAURA. I'm trying to mean it—I'm trying with all my strength.

ALEC. Oh, my dearest dear——

LAURA. Don't—please don't——

MYRTLE (*to the* YOUNG MAN). Fourpence, please.

YOUNG MAN. Thank you. (*He pays, and carries his coffee and sandwich over to the table near the stove.*)

ALBERT. It is all right about to-night, isn't it?

MYRTLE. I'll think about it.

ALBERT. It's Claudette Colbert, you know.

MYRTLE. Fat chance I shall get of enjoying Claudette Colbert with you hissing in me ear all the time.

ALBERT. I'll be as good as gold.

(BERYL *enters* L. *in a coat and hat—she goes behind the counter.*)

ALEC. It's no use running away from the truth, darling—we're lovers, aren't we ? If it happens or if it doesn't, we're lovers in our hearts.

LAURA. Can't you see how wrong it is ? How dreadfully wrong !

ALEC. I can see what's true—whether it's wrong or right.

BERYL (*taking off her hat and coat*). Mr. Saunders wants you, Mr. Godby.

ALBERT. What for ?

BERYL. I don't know.

MYRTLE. You'd better go, Albert ; you know what he is.

ALBERT. I know 'e's a bloody fool, if that's what you mean.

MYRTLE. Be quiet, Albert—in front of Beryl.

BERYL. Don't mind me.

MYRTLE. Go on—finish up your tea.

ALBERT. No peace for the wicked——

MYRTLE. Go on——

ALBERT. I'll be back——

MYRTLE. That'll be nice, I'm sure——

(ALBERT *goes.*)

(MYRTLE *retires to the upper end of the counter.* BERYL *goes off and comes on again laden with various packages of comestibles. She and* MYRTLE *proceed to stack them on the upstage end of the counter.*)

ALEC (*urgently*). There's no chance of Stephen getting back until late—nobody need ever know.

LAURA. It's so furtive to love like that—so cheap— much better not to love at all.

ALEC. It's too late not to love at all—be brave— we're both in the same boat—let's be generous to each other.

LAURA. What is there brave in it—sneaking away to someone else's house, loving in secret with the horror of being found out hanging over us all the time. It would be far braver to say good-bye and never see each other again.

ALEC. Could you be as brave as that? I know I couldn't.

LAURA (*breathlessly*). Couldn't you?

ALEC. Listen, my dear. This is something that's never happened to either of us before. We've loved before and been happy before, and miserable and contented and restless, but this is different—something lovely and strange and desperately difficult. We can't measure it along with the values of our ordinary lives.

LAURA. Why should it be so important—why should we let it be so important?

ALEC. We can't help ourselves.

LAURA. We can—we can if only we're strong enough.

ALEC. Why is it so strong to deny something that's urgent and real—something that all our instincts are straining after—mightn't it be weak and not strong at all to run away from such tremendous longing?

LAURA. Is it so real to you? So tremendous?

ALEC. Can't you see that it is?

LAURA. It's so difficult, so strained. I'm lost.

ALEC. Don't say that, darling.

LAURA. Loving you is hard for me—it makes me a stranger in my own house. Familiar things, ordinary things that I've known for years, like the dining-room curtains, and the wooden tub with a silver top that holds biscuits, and a water-colour of San Remo that my mother painted, look odd to me, as though they belonged to someone else—when I've just left you, when I go home, I'm more lonely than I've ever been before. I passed the house the other day without noticing and had to turn back, and when I went in it seemed to draw away from me—my whole life seems to be drawing away from me, and—and I don't know what to do.

ALEC. Oh, darling——

LAURA. I love them just the same, Fred I mean and the children, but it's as though it wasn't me at all—as though I were looking on at someone else. Do you know what I mean ? Is it the same with you ? or is it easier for men——

ALEC. I don't know.

LAURA. Please, dear, don't look unhappy. I'm not grumbling, really I'm not——

ALEC. I don't suppose being in love has ever been easy for anybody.

LAURA (*reaching for his hand*). We've only got a few more minutes—I didn't mean to be depressing.

ALEC. It isn't any easier for me, darling, honestly it isn't.

LAURA. I know, I know—I only wanted reassuring.

ALEC. I hold you in my arms all the way back in the train—I'm angry with every moment that I'm not alone—to love you uninterrupted—whenever my surgery door opens and a patient comes in, my heart jumps in case it might be you. One of them I'm grateful to—he's got neuritis, and I give him sun-ray treatment—he lies quite quietly baking, and I can be with you in the shadows behind the lamp.

LAURA. How silly we are—how unbearably silly !

ALEC. Friday — Saturday — Sunday — Monday — Tuesday—Wednesday——

LAURA. Thursday——

ALEC. It's all right, isn't it ?

LAURA. Oh, yes—of course it is.

ALEC. Don't pass the house again—don't let it snub you. Go boldly in and stare that damned water-colour out of countenance.

LAURA. All right—don't bake your poor neuritis man too long—you might blister him.

(*The continuation of their scene is drowned by the noisy entrance of two soldiers,* BILL *and* JOHNNIE. *They go to the counter.*)

BILL. Afternoon, lady.

MYRTLE (*grandly*). Good afternoon.

BILL. A couple of splashes, please.

MYRTLE. Very sorry, it's out of hours.

JOHNNIE. Come on, lady—you've got a kind face.

MYRTLE.   That's neither here nor there.

BILL.   Just sneak us a couple under cover of them poor old sandwiches.

MYRTLE.   Them sandwiches were fresh this morning, and I shall do no such thing.

BILL.   Come on, be a sport.

JOHNNIE.   Nobody'd know.

MYRTLE.   I'm very sorry, I'm sure, but it's against the rules.

BILL.   You could pop it into a couple of tea-cups.

MYRTLE.   You're asking me to break the law, young man.

JOHNNIE.   I think I've got a cold coming on—we've been mucking about at the Butts all day—you can't afford to let the army catch cold, you know.

MYRTLE.   You can have as much as you want after six o'clock.

BILL.   An 'eart of stone—that's what you've got, lady —an 'eart of stone.

MYRTLE.   Don't you be cheeky.

JOHNNIE.   My throat's like a parrot's cage—listen ! (*He makes a crackling noise with his throat.*)

MYRTLE.   Take some lemonade, then—or ginger-beer.

BILL.   Couldn't touch it—against doctor's orders— my inside's been most peculiar ever since I 'ad trench feet—you wouldn't give a child carbolic acid, would you ?   That's what ginger-beer does to me.

MYRTLE.   Get on with you !

JOHNNIE.   It's true—it's poison to him, makes 'im make the most 'orrible noises—you wouldn't like anything nasty to 'appen in your posh buffay——

MYRTLE.   May licence does not permit me to serve alcohol out of hours—that's final !

JOHNNIE.   We're soldiers, we are—willing to lay down our lives for you—and you grudge us one splash——

MYRTLE.   You wouldn't want to get me into trouble, would you ?

BILL.   Give us a chance, lady, that's all—just give us a chance.

(*They both roar with laughter.*)

MYRTLE. Beryl, ask Mr. Godby to come 'ere for a moment, will you ?

BERYL. Yes, Mrs. Bagot. (*She comes out from behind the counter and goes on to the platform.*)

BILL. Who's 'e when 'e's at home ?

MYRTLE. You'll soon see—coming in here cheeking me.

JOHNNIE. Now then, now then—naughty naughty

MYRTLE. Kaindly be quiet !

BILL. Shut up, Johnnie——

JOHNNIE. What about them drinks, lady ?

MYRTLE. I've already told you I can't serve alcoholic refreshment out of hours——

JOHNNIE. Come off it, mother, be a pal !

MYRTLE (*losing her temper*). I'll give you mother, you saucy upstart——

BILL. Who are you calling an upstart !

MYRTLE. You—and I'll trouble you to get out of here double quick—disturbing the customers and making a nuisance of yourselves.

JOHNNIE. 'Ere, where's the fire—where's the fire !

(ALBERT GODBY *enters, followed by* BERYL.)

ALBERT. What's going on in 'ere !

MYRTLE (*with dignity*). Mr. Godby, these gentlemen are annoying me.

BILL. We 'aven't done anything.

JOHNNIE. All we did was ask for a couple of drinks

MYRTLE. They insulted me, Mr. Godby.

JOHNNIE. We never did nothing of the sort—just 'aving a little joke, that's all.

ALBERT (*laconically*). 'Op it—both of you.

BILL. We've got a right to stay 'ere as long as we like.

ALBERT. You 'eard what I said—'op it !

JOHNNIE. What is this, a free country or a bloody Sunday school ?

ALBERT (*firmly*). I checked your passes at the gate—your train's due in a minute—Number Two platform—'op it.

JOHNNIE.   Look 'ere, now——

BILL.   Come on, Johnnie—don't argue with the poor little basket.

ALBERT (*dangerously*).   'Op it !

(BILL *and* JOHNNIE *go to the door*—JOHNNIE *turns*.)

JOHNNIE.   Toodle-oo, mother, and if them sandwiches were made this morning, you're Shirley Temple——

(*They go out*.)

MYRTLE.   Thank you, Albert.

BERYL.   What a nerve, talking to you like that !

MYRTLE.   Be quiet, Beryl—pour me out a nip of Three Star—I'm feeling quite upset.

ALBERT.   I've got to get back to the gate.

MYRTLE (*graciously*).   I'll be seeing you later, Albert.

ALBERT (*with a wink*).   Okay !

(*He goes out*.)

(*A train bell rings.* BERYL *brings* MYRTLE *a glass of brandy.*)

MYRTLE (*sipping it*).   I'll say one thing for Albert Godby—he may be on the small side, but 'e's a gentleman.

(*She and* BERYL *retire once more to the upper end of the counter and continue their arrangement of bottles, biscuits, etc.   There is the sound of a train drawing into the station.*)

LAURA.   There's your train.

ALEC.   I'm going to miss it.

LAURA.   Please go.

ALEC.   No.

LAURA (*clasping and unclasping her hands*).   I wish I could think clearly.   I wish I could know—really know what to do.

ALEC.   Do you trust me ?

LAURA.   Yes—I trust you.

ALEC.   I don't mean conventionally—I mean really.

LAURA.   Yes.

ALEC. Everything's against us—all the circumstances of our lives—those have got to go on unaltered. We're nice people, you and I, and we've got to go on being nice. Let's enclose this love of ours with real strength, and let that strength be that no one is hurt by it except ourselves.

LAURA. Must we be hurt by it ?

ALEC. Yes—when the time comes.

LAURA. Very well.

ALEC. All the furtiveness and the secrecy and the hole-in-corner cheapness can be justified if only we're strong enough—strong enough to keep it to ourselves, clean and untouched by anybody else's knowledge or even suspicions—something of our own for ever—to be remembered——

LAURA. Very well.

ALEC. We won't speak of it any more—I'm going now—back to Stephen's flat. I'll wait for you—if you don't come I shall know only that you weren't quite ready—that you needed a little longer to find your own dear heart. This is the address.

(*He scribbles on a bit of paper as the express thunders through the station. He gets up and goes swiftly without looking at her again. She sits staring at the paper, then she fumbles in her bag and finds a cigarette. She lights it—the platform bell goes.*)

MYRTLE. There's the five forty-three.

BERYL. We ought to have another Huntley and Palmer's to put in the middle, really.

MYRTLE. There are some more on the shelf.

(BERYL *fetches another packet of biscuits and takes it to* MYRTLE. *There is the noise of the* 5.43—LAURA'S *train —steaming into the station.* LAURA *sits puffing her cigarette. Suddenly she gets up—gathers up her bag quickly, and moves towards the door. She pauses and comes back to the table as the whistle blows. The train starts, she puts the paper in her bag and goes quietly out as the lights fade.*)

SCENE IV

*The time is about 9.45 p.m. on an evening in December.
There are only two lights on in the refreshment-room
as it is nearly closing time.*

When the SCENE *starts the stage is empty. There is the
noise of a fast train rattling through the station.*

BERYL *comes in from the upstage door behind the
counter armed with several muslin cloths which she proceeds to drape over the things on the counter. She hums
breathily to herself as she does so.* STANLEY *enters. He
has discarded his uniform and is wearing his ordinary
clothes.*

STANLEY. Hallo !

BERYL. You made me jump.

STANLEY. Are you walking home ?

BERYL. Maybe.

STANLEY. Do you want me to wait ?

BERYL. I've got to go straight back.

STANLEY. Why ?

BERYL. Mother'll be waiting up.

STANLEY. Can't you say you've been kept late ?

BERYL. I said that last time.

STANLEY. Say it again—say there's been a rush
on.

BERYL. Don't be so silly—Mother's not that much
of a fool.

STANLEY. Be a sport, Beryl—shut down five minutes
early and say you was kept ten minutes late—that gives
us a quarter of an hour.

BERYL. What happens if Mrs. Bagot comes back ?

STANLEY. She won't—she's out having a bit of a slap
and tickle with our Albert.

BERYL. Stan, you are awful !

STANLEY. I'll wait for you in the yard.

BERYL. Oh, all right.

(STANLEY *goes out.*)

(BERYL *resumes her song and the draping of the cake-stands.*
   LAURA *enters—she looks pale and unhappy.*)

LAURA.   I'd like a glass of brandy, please.

BERYL.   We're just closing.

LAURA.   I see you are, but you're not quite closed
yet, are you ?

BERYL (*sullenly*).   Three Star ?

LAURA.   Yes, that'll do.

BERYL (*getting it*).   Tenpence, please.

LAURA (*taking money from her bag*).   Here—and—
have you a piece of paper and an envelope ?

BERYL.   I'm afraid you'll have to get that at the
bookstall.

LAURA.   The bookstall's shut—please—it's very important—I should be so much obliged——

BERYL.   Oh, all right—wait a minute.

(*She goes off.* LAURA *sips the brandy at the counter;
   she is obviously trying to control her nerves.* BERYL
   returns with some notepaper and an envelope.)

LAURA.   Thank you so much.

BERYL.   We close in a few minutes, you know.

LAURA.   Yes, I know.

(*She takes the notepaper and her brandy over to the table
   below the door and sits down. She stares at the paper
   for a moment, takes another sip of brandy and then
   begins to write.* BERYL *looks at her with exasperation
   and goes off through the upstage door* R. LAURA *falters
   in her writing, then breaks down and buries her face in
   her hands.* ALEC *comes in—he looks hopelessly round
   for a moment, and then sees her.*)

ALEC.   Thank God—oh, darling !

LAURA.   Please go away—please don't say anything.

ALEC.   I can't leave you like this.

LAURA.   You must.   It'll be better—really it will.

ALEC (*sitting down beside her*).   You're being dreadfully cruel.

LAURA.   I feel so utterly degraded.

ALEC.   It was just a beastly accident that he came

back early—he doesn't know who you are—he never
even saw you.

LAURA.   I listened to your voices in the sitting-room—
I crept out and down the stairs—feeling like a prostitute.

ALEC.   Don't, dearest—don't talk like that, please

LAURA (*bitterly*).   I suppose he laughed, didn't he—
after he got over being annoyed ?   I suppose you spoke
of me together as men of the world.

ALEC.   We didn't speak of you—we spoke of a name-
less creature who had no reality at all.

LAURA (*wildly*).   Why didn't you tell him the truth ?
Why didn't you say who I was and that we were lovers
—shameful secret lovers—using his flat like a bad
house because we had nowhere else to go, and were
afraid of being found out !   Why didn't you tell him
we were cheap and low and without courage—why didn't
you—— ?

ALEC.   Stop it, Laura—pull yourself together !

LAURA.   It's true—don't you see, it's true !

ALEC.   It's nothing of the sort.   I know you feel
horrible, and I'm deeply, desperately sorry.   I feel
horrible, too, but it doesn't matter really—this—this
unfortunate, damnable incident—it was just bad luck.
It couldn't affect us really, you and me—we know the
truth—we know we really love each other—*that's* all
that matters.

LAURA.   It isn't all that matters—other things matter
too, self-respect matters, and decency—I can't go on
any longer.

ALEC.   Could you really—say good-bye—not see me
any more ?

LAURA.   Yes—if you'd help me.

(*There is silence for a moment.*   ALEC *gets up and walks
about—he stops and stands staring at a coloured calendar
on the wall.*)

ALEC (*quietly, with his back to her*).   I love you, Laura
—I shall love you always until the end of my life—all
     shame that the world might force on us couldn't

touch the real truth of it. I can't look at you now because I know something—I know that this is the beginning of the end—not the end of my loving you —but the end of our being together. But not quite yet, darling—please not quite yet.

LAURA. Very well—not quite yet.

ALEC. I know what you feel—about this evening, I mean—about the beastliness of it. I know about the strain of our different lives, our lives apart from each other. The feeling of guilt—of doing wrong is a little too strong, isn't it ? Too persistent—perhaps too great a price to pay for the few hours of happiness we get out of it. I know all this because it's the same for me too.

LAURA. You can look at me now—I'm all right.

ALEC (*turning*). Let's be careful—let's prepare ourselves—a sudden break now, however brave and admirable, would be too cruel—we can't do such violence to our hearts and minds.

LAURA. Very well.

ALEC. I'm going away.

LAURA. I see.

ALEC. But not quite yet.

LAURA. Please not quite yet.

(BERYL *enters in hat and coat.*)

BERYL. I'm afraid it's closing time.

ALEC. Oh, is it ?

BERYL. I shall have to lock up.

ALEC. This lady is catching the ten-ten—she's not feeling very well, and it's very cold on the platform.

BERYL. The waiting-room's open.

ALEC (*going to the counter*). Look here—I'd be very much obliged if you'd let us stay here for another few minutes.

BERYL. I'm sorry—it's against the rules.

ALEC (*giving her a ten-shilling note*). Please—come back to lock up when the train comes in.

BERYL. I'll have to switch off the lights—someone might see 'em on and think we were open.

ALEC. Just for a few minutes—please !

BERYL. You won't touch anything, will you ?

ALEC. Not a thing.

BERYL. Oh, all right.

(*She switches off the lights. The lamp from the platform shines in through the window so it isn't quite dark.*)

ALEC. Thank you very much.

(BERYL *goes out by the platform door, closing it behind her.*)

LAURA. Just a few minutes.

ALEC. Let's have a cigarette, shall we ?

LAURA. I have some. (*She takes her bag up from the table.*)

ALEC (*producing his case*). No, here. (*He lights their cigarettes carefully.*) Now then—I want you to promise me something.

LAURA. What is it ?

ALEC. Promise me that however unhappy you are, and however much you think things over, that you'll meet me next Thursday as usual.

LAURA. Not at the flat.

ALEC. No—be at the Picture House Café at the same time. I'll hire a car—we'll drive out into the country.

LAURA. All right—I promise.

ALEC. We've got to talk—I've got to explain.

LAURA. About going away ?

ALEC. Yes.

LAURA. Where are you going ? Where *can* you go ? You *can't* give up your practice !

ALEC. I've had a job offered me—I wasn't going to tell you—I wasn't going to take it—I know now, it's the only way out.

LAURA. Where ?

ALEC. A long way away—Johannesburg.

LAURA (*hopelessly*). Oh, God !

ALEC (*hurriedly*). My brother's out there—they're opening a new hospital—they want me in it. It's a fine opportunity, really. I'll take Madeleine and the boys, it's been torturing me for three weeks, the necessity of making a decision one way or the other—I haven't told anybody, not even Madeleine. I couldn't bear the idea of leaving you, but now I see—it's got to happen soon, anyway—it's almost happening already.

LAURA (*tonelessly*). When will you go?

ALEC. In about two months' time.

LAURA. It's quite near, isn't it?

ALEC. Do you want me to stay? Do you want me to turn down the offer?

LAURA. Don't be foolish, Alec.

ALEC. I'll do whatever you say.

LAURA. That's unkind of you, my darling. (*She suddenly buries her head in her arms and bursts into tears.*)

ALEC (*putting his arms round her*). Oh, Laura, don't, please don't!

LAURA. I'll be all right—leave me alone a minute.

ALEC. I love you—I love you.

LAURA. I know.

ALEC. We knew we'd get hurt.

LAURA (*sitting up*). I'm being very stupid.

ALEC (*giving her his handkerchief*). Here.

LAURA (*blowing her nose*). Thank you.

(*The platform bell goes.*)

There's my train.

ALEC. You're not angry with me, are you?

LAURA. No, I'm not angry—I don't think I'm anything, really—I feel just tired.

ALEC. Forgive me.

LAURA. Forgive you for what?

ALEC. For everything—for having met you in the first place—for taking the piece of grit out of your eye—for loving you—for bringing you so much misery.

LAURA (*trying to smile*). I'll forgive you—if you'll forgive me——

(*There is the noise of a train pulling into the station.* BERYL *enters.* LAURA *and* ALEC *get up.*)

ALEC. I'll see you into the train.

LAURA. No—please stay here.

(*She rises and goes to* ALEC *and embraces him.*)

ALEC.   All right.

LAURA (*softly*).   Good night, darling.

(*She goes hurriedly out on to the platform without looking back.*)

ALEC.   The last train for Churley hasn't gone yet, has it ?

BERYL.   I couldn't say, I'm sure.   I must lock up now.

ALEC.   All right.   I'll wait in the waiting-room— thank you very much.   Good night.

BERYL.   Good night.

(*The train starts as he goes out on to the platform.* BERYL *locks the door carefully after him, and then goes off up-stage* R. *as the lights fade.*)

SCENE V

The time is between 5 and 5.30 on an afternoon in March.

MYRTLE *is behind the counter.* BERYL *is crouching over the stove putting coals in it.* ALBERT *enters.*

ALBERT (*gaily*).   One tea, please—two lumps of sugar, and a Bath bun, and make it snappy.

MYRTLE.   What's the matter with you ?

ALBERT.   Beryl, 'op it.

MYRTLE.   Don't you go ordering Beryl about—you haven't any right to.

ALBERT.   You heard me, Beryl—'op it.

BERYL (*giggling*).   Well, I never !

MYRTLE.   Go into the back room a minute, Beryl.

BERYL.   Yes, Mrs. Bagot.

(*She goes.*)

MYRTLE.   Now then, Albert—you behave—we don't want the whole station laughing at us.

ALBERT.   What is there to laugh at ?

MYRTLE.   Here's your tea.

ALBERT. How d'you feel ?

MYRTLE. Don't talk so soft—how should I feel ?

ALBERT. I only wondered—— (*He leans towards her.*)

MYRTLE. Look out—somebody's coming in.

ALBERT. It's only Romeo and Juliet.

(LAURA *and* ALEC *come in.* LAURA *goes to the same table,* ALEC *to the counter.*)

ALEC. Good afternoon.

MYRTLE. Good afternoon—same as usual !

ALEC. Yes, please.

MYRTLE (*drawing tea*). Quite springy out, isn't it !

ALEC. Yes—quite.

(*He pays her, collects the tea and carries it over to the table—something in his manner causes* ALBERT *to make a grimace over his teacup at* MYRTLE. ALEC *sits down at the table, and he and* LAURA *sip their tea in silence.*)

ALBERT. I spoke to Mr. Saunders.

MYRTLE. What did he say ?

ALBERT. 'E was very decent, as a matter-of-fact—said it'd be all right——

(MILDRED *comes in hurriedly. She is a fair girl wearing a station overall.*)

MILDRED. Is Beryl here ?

MYRTLE. Why, Mildred, whatever's the matter ?

MILDRED. It's her mother—she's bad again—they telephoned through to the booking office.

MYRTLE. She's inside—you'd better go in. Don't go yelling it at her, now—tell her gently.

MILDRED. They said she'd better come at once.

MYRTLE. I thought this was going to happen—stay here, Mildred. I'll tell her. Wait a minute, Albert.

(MYRTLE *vanishes into the inside room.*)

ALBERT. Better get back to the bookstall, hadn't you ?

MILDRED. Do you think she's going to die ?

ALBERT. How do I know ?

MILDRED. Mr. Saunders thinks she is—judging by what the doctor said on the telephone.

ALBERT. 'Ow do you know it was the doctor ?

MILDRED. Mr. Saunders said it was.

ALBERT. She's always being took bad, that old woman.

MILDRED. Do you think Beryl would like me to go along with her ?

ALBERT. You can't, and leave nobody on the papers.

MILDRED. Mr. Saunders said I might if it was necessary.

ALBERT. Well, go and get your 'at then, and don't make such a fuss.

(MYRTLE *comes back.*)

MYRTLE. She's going at once, poor little thing !

ALBERT. Mildred's going with her.

MYRTLE. All right, Mildred—go on.

MILDRED (*half-way to the door*). What about me 'at ?

MYRTLE. Never mind about your 'at—go this way.

(MILDRED *rushes off up stage* R.)

Poor child—this has been hanging over her for weeks. (*She puts her head round the door.*) Mildred, tell Beryl she needn't come back to-night, I'll stay on.

ALBERT. 'Ere, you can't do that, we was going to the Broadway Melody of Nineteen Thirty-six.

MYRTLE. For shame, Albert—thinking of the Broadway Melody of Nineteen Thirty-six in a moment of life and death !

ALBERT. But look 'ere, Myrtle——

MYRTLE. I dreamt of a hearse last night, and whenever I dream of a hearse something happens—you mark my words——

ALBERT. I've got reserved tickets——

MYRTLE. Send Stanley to change them on his way home. Come in 'ere when you go off and I'll make you a little supper inside.

ALBERT (*grumbily*). Everybody getting into a state and fussing about——

MYRTLE. You shock me, Albert, you do really—go on, finish up your tea and get back to the gate.

(*She turns and goes to the upper end of the counter.* ALBERT *gulps his tea.*)

ALBERT (*slamming the cup down on the counter*). Women !

(*He stamps out on to the platform.*)

ALEC. Are you all right, darling ?

LAURA. Yes, I'm all right.

ALEC. I wish I could think of something to say.

LAURA. It doesn't matter—not saying anything, I mean.

ALEC. I'll miss my train and wait to see you into yours.

LAURA. No—no—please don't. I'll come over to your platform with you—I'd rather.

ALEC. Very well.

LAURA. Do you think we shall ever see each other again ?

ALEC. I don't know. (*His voice breaks.*) Not for years, anyway.

LAURA. The children will all be grown up—I wonder if they'll ever meet and know each other.

ALEC. Couldn't I write to you—just once in a while ?

LAURA. No—please not—we promised we wouldn't.

ALEC. Please know this—please know that you'll be with me for ages and ages yet—far away into the future. Time will wear down the agony of not seeing you, bit by bit the pain will go—but the loving you and the memory of you won't ever go—please know that.

LAURA. I know it.

ALEC. It's easier for me than for you. I do realize that, really I do. I at least will have different shapes to look at, and new work to do—you have to go on among familiar things—my heart aches for you so.

LAURA. I'll be all right.

ALEC. I love you with all my heart and soul.

LAURA (*quietly*). I want to die—if only I could die.

ALEC. If you died you'd forget me—I want to be remembered.

LAURA. Yes, I know—I do too.

ALEC. Good-bye, my dearest love.

LAURA. Good-bye, my dearest love.

ALEC. We've still got a few minutes.

LAURA. Thank God—— !

(DOLLY MESSITER *bustles into the refreshment-room. She is a nicely dressed woman, with rather a fussy manner. She is laden with parcels. She sees* LAURA.)

DOLLY. Laura ! What a lovely surprise !

LAURA (*dazed*). Oh, Dolly !

DOLLY. My dear, I've been shopping till I'm dropping ! My feet are nearly falling off, and my throat's parched. I thought of having tea in Spindle's, but I was terrified of losing the train. I'm always missing trains, and being late for meals, and Bob gets disagreeable for days at a time. Oh, dear—— (*She flops down at their table.*)

LAURA. This is Doctor Harvey.

ALEC (*rising*). How do you do !

DOLLY (*shaking hands*). How do you do ! Would you be a perfect dear and get me a cup of tea ! I don't think I could drag my poor old bones as far as the counter. I must get some chocolates for Tony, too, but I can do that afterwards. (*She offers him money.*)

ALEC (*waving it away*). No, please——

(*He goes drearily over to the counter, gets another cup of tea from* MYRTLE, *pays for it and comes back to the table. Meanwhile* DOLLY *continues to talk.*)

DOLLY. My dear—what a nice-looking man. Who on earth is he ? Really, you're quite a dark horse. I shall telephone Fred in the morning and make mischief —that is a bit of luck. I haven't seen you for ages, and I've been meaning to pop in, but Tony's had measles,

you know, and I had all that awful fuss about Phyllis—
but of course you don't know—she left me!

LAURA (*with an effort*). Oh, how dreadful!

DOLLY. Mind you, I never cared for her much, but
still Tony did. Tony adored her, and—but, never mind,
I'll tell you all about that in the train.

(ALEC *arrives back at the table with her tea—he sits down
again.*)

Thank you so very much. They've certainly put enough
milk in it—but still, it'll be refreshing. (*She sips it.*)
Oh, dear—no sugar.

ALEC. It's in the spoon.

DOLLY. Oh, of course—what a fool I am—Laura, you
look frightfully well. I do wish I'd known you were
coming in to-day, we could have come together and
lunched and had a good gossip. I loathe shopping by
myself, anyway.

(*There is the sound of a bell on the platform.*)

LAURA. There's your train.

ALEC. Yes, I know.

DOLLY. Aren't you coming with us?

ALEC. No, I go in the opposite direction. My practice is in Churley.

DOLLY. Oh, I see.

ALEC. I'm a general practitioner at the moment.

LAURA (*dully*). Doctor Harvey is going out to Africa
next week.

DOLLY. Oh! how thrilling.

(*There is the sound of* ALEC'S *train approaching.*)

ALEC. I must go.

LAURA. Yes, you must.

ALEC. Good-bye.

DOLLY. Good-bye.

(*He shakes hands with* DOLLY, *looks at* LAURA *swiftly
once, then presses her hand under cover of the table and
leaves hurriedly as the train is heard rumbling into the
station.* LAURA *sits quite still.*)

He'll have to run—he's got to get right over to the other platform. How did you meet him ?

LAURA. I got something in my eye one day, and he took it out.

DOLLY. My dear—how very romantic ! I'm always getting things in my eye and nobody the least bit attractive has ever paid the faintest attention—which reminds me—you know about Harry and Lucy Jenner, don't you ?

LAURA (*listening for the train to start*). No—what about them ?

DOLLY. My dear—they're going to get a divorce—at least, I believe they're getting a conjugal separation, or whatever it is, to begin with, and the divorce later on.

(*The train starts, and the sound of it gradually dies away in the distance.*)

It seems that there's an awful Mrs. Something or other in London that he's been carrying on with for ages—you know how he was always having to go up on business. Well, apparently Lucy's sister saw them, Harry and this woman, in the Tate Gallery of all places, and she wrote to Lucy, and then gradually the whole thing came out. Of course, it was all most disgraceful. To begin with, I think it was a dirty trick to make such a fuss openly— it might have been smoothed over perfectly easily and no one would have known anything about it.

(*There is the sound of a bell on the platform.*)

Is that our train ? (*She addresses* MYRTLE.) Can you tell me, is that the Ketchworth train ?

MYRTLE. No, that's the express.

LAURA. The boat train.

DOLLY. Oh, yes—that doesn't stop, does it ? Express trains are Tony's passion in life—he knows them all by name—where they start from and where they go to, and how long they take to get there. Oh, dear, I mustn't forget his chocolate.

(*She jumps up and goes to the counter.* LAURA *remains quite still.*)

(*At the counter.*) I want some chocolate, please.

MYRTLE. Milk or plain ?

DOLLY. Plain, I think—or no, perhaps milk would be nicer. Have you any with nuts in it ?

(*The express is heard in the distance.*)

MYRTLE. Nestlé's nut-milk—shilling or sixpence ?

DOLLY. Give me one plain and one nut-milk.

(*The noise of the express sounds louder—LAURA suddenly gets up and goes swiftly out on to the platform. The express roars through the station as DOLLY finishes buying and paying for her chocolate. She turns.*)

Oh ! where is she ?

MYRTLE (*looking over the counter*). I never noticed her go.

(DOLLY *comes over to the table.* LAURA *comes in again, looking very white and shaky.*)

DOLLY. My dear, I couldn't think where you'd disappeared to.

LAURA. I just wanted to see the express go through.

DOLLY. What on earth's the matter—do you feel ill ?

LAURA. I feel a little sick.

DOLLY. Have you any brandy ?

MYRTLE. I'm afraid it's out of hours.

DOLLY. Surely—if someone's feeling ill——

LAURA. I'm all right, really.

(*The platform bell goes.*)

That's our train.

DOLLY. Just a sip of brandy will buck you up. (*To* MYRTLE.) Please——

MYRTLE. Very well.

(*She pours out some brandy.*)

DOLLY. How much ?

MYRTLE. Tenpence, please.

DOLLY (*paying her*). There ! (*She takes the brandy*

over to LAURA, *who has sat down again at the table*.)   Here
you are, dear.

LAURA (*taking it*).   Thank you.

As she sips it, the train is heard coming into the station.
DOLLY *proceeds to gather up her parcels as*

The CURTAIN *falls.*

FURNITURE AND PROPERTY PLOT

FURNITURE

2 two-shelved tin mirrors.
Curved counter.
3 iron tables.
3 tops to them.
Stove
12 bentwood chairs.
High stool.

PROPERTIES

On Counter.

2 bar handles.
Two-shelfed glass stand with vase of flowers on top, bearin
   apples, bananas and packets of biscuits.
2 glass-covered stands.
Bath buns and rock-cakes in one up **B.**
Sandwiches (one edible) in the other.
12 cups and saucers.
4 sugar-basins.
4 milk-jugs.
24 glasses.
12 small plates.
6 teaspoons.
Tin tea urn.
3 brown teapots.
Jug of water (advert.).
1 large plate of Banburys.
Bottle of biscuits (advert.).
2 ashtrays (advert.).
Dummy packets of chocolates.

Under Counter.

4 muslin cloths to cover counter and shelves.
3 dishcloths on pegs.
Jug of Coffee (Scene **3**).
Drawer-till with bell.
Money in till.
3 tin trays (adverts.).
   1 with 6 Cadbury's and paper and pencil on.

46

On Lower Shelf behind Counter.
Bottle of Three Star Brandy and measure.
Dressing (adverts.).

On Upper Shelf behind Counter.
Dressing (adverts.).

On Upper Shelf at end of Counter.
False shelf dressed.

On Lower Shelf at end of Counter.
False shelf dressed.

On Centre Table.
Evening paper.
Cup of tea.
Water-bottle.
Vase of flowers.

By Stove.
Scuttle.
Shovel.
Poker.

On Upstage Table L.
Bottle.
Vase of flowers.
Matchstand and ashtray.
Crumbs.

On Downstage Table L.
Library book.
Cup of tea.
Vase of flowers.
Matchstand and ashtray.
Two Coathangers.
Framed bill of fare.
Framed advertisements.

Off R.
Envelopes and sheet of notepaper.
Tray of shelf dressing.
Broom.

Off L.
Guard's whistle.
Cylinder of oxygen.
Slung tray of chocolates and cigarettes.
6 yellow roses.
4 shopping parcels.
2 dirty cups and saucers.
" The Lancet."

Door-bang (lying on the ground).
10*s.* note.
3 crates.
1 basket.
Valises.

Dressing.

Packets of Gold Flake, Capstan, Woodbines, Players, Bachelors.
Packets of Nestlé's, Cadbury.
Packets of Huntley and Palmer's—Maries.
Bottles of Idris, Black and White, Johnny Walker, Schweppes, Whitbreads.
Model advertisements.
Standing advertisements.
Hanging advertisements.
Dummies on shelves glued on and in slung tray.

Changes.

End of Scene 1.—Clear tables. Milk in 3 cups.
End of Scene 2.—Clear tables, false shelves, teapots. Counter up. Coffee on. Milk in 3 cups. Light switches down. Behind-counter door open.
End of Scene 3.—Clear tables.
End of Scene 4.—Clear tables. Muslin covers. Counter up. Milk in 3 cups.

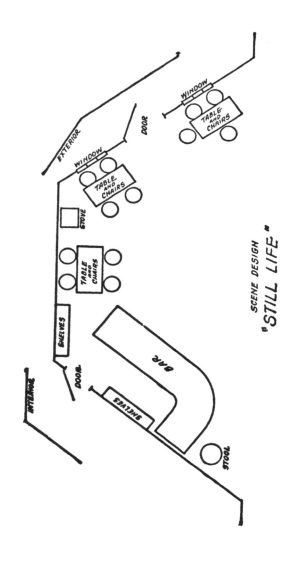

SCENE DESIGN
"STILL LIFE"

Also By

Noël Coward

THE ASTONISHED HEART
BLITHE SPIRIT
CONVERSATION PIECE
COWARDY CUSTARD
DESIGN FOR LIVING
EASY VIRTUE
FALLEN ANGELS
HAY FEVER
I'LL LEAVE IT TO YOU
LOOK AFTER LULU
THE MARQUISE
NOEL COWARD IN TWO KEYS
NUDE WITH VIOLIN
PEACE IN OUR TIME
PRESENT LAUGHTER
PRIVATE LIVES
QUADRILLE
RELATIVE VALUES
SHADOW PLAY
A SONG AT TWILIGHT
THIS HAPPY BREED
THIS WAS A MAN
TONIGHT AT 8:30
THE VORTEX
WAITING IN THE WINGS
THE YOUNG IDEA

SAMUELFRENCH.COM

OTHER TITLES AVAILABLE FROM SAMUEL FRENCH

THE ASTONISHED HEART
Noël Coward

Play / 4m, 3f / Interior
One of the *Tonight at 8:30* series produced in London and
New York. In psychiatrist Christian Faber's drawing room sits
his weeping wife and his sad assistants, waiting for the siren
Leonora. In four flashbacks the story emerges: Leonora, a
girlhood chum, visited Christian's wife and was introduced
to him. She set out to capture her friend's husband but was
captured herself. She threw him over because of his jealousy.
He jumped out of the window. Leonora has come because
Christian calls for her on his death bed. She returns slowly
from his room to announce he has died and that his last words
were tender ones to his wife, for whom he mistook Leonora.
Also published in *Tonight at 8:30*.

OTHER TITLES AVAILABLE FROM SAMUEL FRENCH

SAME TIME, NEXT YEAR
Bernard Slade

Comedy / 1m, 1f / Interior
One of the most popular romantic comedies of the century, *Same Time, Next Year* ran four years on Broadway, winning a Tony Award for lead actress Ellen Burstyn, who later recreated her role in the successful motion picture. It remains one of the world's most widely produced plays. The plot follows a love affair between two people, Doris and George, married to others, who rendezvous once a year. Twenty-five years of manners and morals are hilariously and touchingly played out by the lovers.

"Delicious wit, compassion, a sense of humor and a feel for nostalgia."
– *The New York Times*

"Genuinely funny and genuinely romantic."
– *The New York Post*

OTHER TITLES AVAILABLE FROM SAMUEL FRENCH

TAKE HER, SHE'S MINE
Phoebe and Henry Ephron

Comedy / 11m, 6f / Various Sets

Art Carney and Phyllis Thaxter played the Broadway roles of parents of two typical American girls enroute to college. The story is based on the wild and wooly experiences the authors had with their daughters, Nora Ephron and Delia Ephron, themselves now well known writers. The phases of a girl's life are cause for enjoyment except to fearful fathers. Through the first two years, the authors tell us, college girls are frightfully sophisticated about all departments of human life. Then they pass into the "liberal" period of causes and humanitarianism, and some into the intellectual lethargy of beatniksville. Finally, they start to think seriously of their lives as grown ups. It's an experience in growing up, as much for the parents as for the girls.

"A warming comedy. A delightful play about parents vs kids. It's loaded with laughs. It's going to be a smash hit."
– *New York Mirror*

Lightning Source UK Ltd.
Milton Keynes UK
UKOW06f0133081015

260059UK00008B/100/P

9 780573 624902